# Road to the White House

### A candidate who knows the angles yet speaks in circles

## Paul Mellor

All rights reserved. No part of this book shall be reproduced or transmitted in any form or by any means, electronic, mechanical, magnetic, photographic including photocopying, recording or by any information storage and retrieval system, without prior written permission of the publisher. No patent liability is assumed with respect to the use of the information contained herein. Although every precaution has been taken in the preparation of this book, the publisher and author assume no responsibility for errors or omissions. Neither is any liability assumed for damages resulting from the use of the information contained herein.

Copyright © 2018 by Paul Mellor

ISBN 978-0692170854

# An Open Letter to the American People

My name is Paul Mellor and I'm running for the Presidency of the United States of America.

I decided to pursue the highest office in the land after consulting with my cousin Robbie, two of my friends who I located on Facebook, and from a hitchhiker I picked up on Highway 20 during a torrential hailstorm in eastern Oregon.

I revisited this decision with my wife of nine years, my girlfriend of three months, my pastor, my candlestick maker, and my Irish baker whom I met on a Norwegian fishing trip in 1975. They all said the same thing: It's time.

Yes, my fellow countrymen, it is time. It's time to take America back to its values, its core beliefs, and to its origin when men were men, boys were boys, and when the Indians were atop the American League East.

I stand for many things; human rights, equal rights, and right hand turns after coming to a complete stop. I believe in that; always have. Always will.

I believe in tradition, such as autumn leaves, rainbow trout, and standing back from the yellow line when you hear the bells and whistles of an approaching train coming from the bowels of New York City. I believe in that.

I believe in horse racing, and auto racing, and all the other kinds of racisms such as the 5K, the 10K, and the half marathons that take place throughout this country. I believe in that.

Friends, I come from humble beginnings. I was born in Tyler, Texas at a time when I couldn't read.

I studied hard in school and was well-liked. I won "*Most Popular 7th Grader*" 3 years in a row.

Daddy taught me the value of hard work at an early age. He showed me how to pick cotton even though I was afraid of heights.

He taught me about honesty, integrity, and doing what's right, which I was able to share with my buddies at Belmont Correctional School for Boys.

Mother was a wonderful woman. She would spend time feeding and bathing me. They were truly the best 25 years of my life.

But now I hear America's voice. So please, help me help you so we all can help ourselves to what we rightly deserve, including all the nice stuff our neighbors have.

Friends, I've often been asked what made me decide to run for the Office of the Presidency. My answer is simple, yet complex.

After being turned down from one job after another because of what, some may say, lack of experience, I learned about another job that fit my qualifications:

*Born in the USA and be in your mid-thirties*

The position provided free housing, free meals, and a deep love for this country. Friends, I was hungry to get started.

Over the past several months, I have traveled this great country of ours taking a pulse of this nation. From Montgomery to Montreal, from Terre Haute to Tijuana, and from Vicksburg to Vancouver Island, I have listened to ordinary Americans share their hopes and dreams for a better tomorrow.

On the following pages, I take you, the reader, into those town halls and coffee shops where I hear the concerns of our citizens. I offer solutions and a vision for a better way of life.

I thank you for taking this journey with me, and I ask for your support come November so that together, you and me (or is it ... you and I) can make this country strong and prosperous, and that we all can be happy, because in the end, isn't that what we want?

God Bless,

*Paul*

Paul Mellor

One may say it would be difficult to not thank the people who have paved the path for one's success. I'm not like that. All the success I have achieved has come from my efforts.

(On to page 7)

Tuesday, February 1, 12:09pm
Chatterbox Café
Harlan, Iowa

## Q & A session with waitress Rochelle

**Q:** Excuse me Sir, can you move? You're really getting in my way.

**A:** Okay. I'm sorry.

Monday, December 18, 7:35pm
American Legion Post
Marietta, Georgia

## Q & A session with Veterans

**Q:** **What are your initial views on the Trade Bill?**

**A:** This is something that comes naturally to me. It's all about buying American goods.

When I needed to buy new tires, I didn't take it to some foreign dealer. No, I bought Goodyear, American made, and have been very pleased with my purchase. In fact, I think my Toyota runs much better. The batteries for my camera and radio are also made here in America. The Sony and Nikon don't know the difference.

Our elected officials aren't doing enough in this area. Many of them go off to faraway places for meetings or vacations pumping money into that country's economy. Recently, they're traveled to Rio de Janeiro, Monte Carlo, and Hawaii. What's wrong with this country, I say.

One of the ways we can accomplish a balanced trade agreement is if we decrease domestic spending. How do we do that? Quite simply, we must reposition our tax system.

Presently, 17% of our annual income goes directly into GNP. Those figures come from OMB, which began under FDR when the WPA began. I propose we change that.

During a recent luncheon at P.F. Chang's while sipping an RC Cola, CEO's from DHL, CVS, IBM, and AIG, all told me the same thing: Change the tax code ASAP.

Of course, the IRS won't like that and I'm sure the ACLU will object, too. But the facts speak for themselves.

11% of social security benefits are funneled into health insurance, mostly HMO's, according to an AARP study in LA. They learned after looking at a report on TV done by the BBC, that income generated by MD's in the UK produce a net profit back into the government. The same study done at UCLA found that it could be done in the US, as well. Therefore, this money could be invested into CD's or IRA's or 401K's, so says the GOP, which would cover the FDIC tax. If this had been done in the 60's under LBJ, the TVA would have received greater power and AT&T wouldn't have the competition that it faces today. Of course, the AFL-CIO has its opinion.

I'm no genius. I do not have a PhD, which wouldn't surprise you if you saw my SAT's, but I do have an intuition, call it ESP if you will.

CPA's all agree that less taxes creates more R&D for industries and more R&R for our fellow Americans. Thus, freeing up time for leisure activities, such as taking in more NBA, NFL, or NHL games or working out at the YMCA. Some, on the other hand, may want to hang around the house in their PJ's, while others, according to AAA, will want to travel from C to C.

Higher taxes prevent this. It was proven in what was then the USSR. People didn't have enough money to eat. Many of them could only afford M&M's and A&W Root Beer. We learned this from the CIA, which was later confirmed by the KGB.

Last week, CNN reported that since the passage of the GI Bill more Americans are getting an education on this very important issue. And this is good. PTA membership is up, and people are beginning to fight back. Of course, this doesn't mean that we should call in ATF agents or sign up for NRA membership, nor does it mean that we should call in the dogs which the SPCA wouldn't mind. What it does mean is that we should contact our elected officials in DC, OK?

Saturday, January 27, 10:14am
Jane's Latvian Dress Shop for Girls and Boys
Point Roberts, Washington

## Q & A session with Patrons

**Q:** **How will you protect the environment?**

**A:** The environment is all around us. You'll see it at home, at work, and along river banks in inner cities. I was introduced to the environment as a youth when my family traveled out west to California, and I enjoyed the environment very much. Years later, at a college fraternity party, I was introduced to it again, and I must say, the environment that night was very good.

As Americans in search of truth, it's important that we protect the environment. That's why if elected, I will build an environmental research center in what is now Yellowstone National Park.

This facility will employ roughly 4000 people who will help find ways on how to improve the way we live. I'm excited about this project. Already, plans have begun as to where land will be cleared and where new roads will be laid down.

On the following page is my environmentalist spelling out my position on this very important issue.

## **Environmenta List**

1. When given the choice between paper or plastic, it's important that the fundamental decision we make be the right one.

2. When refueling our automobiles, it's important that the petroleum we use be antitoxin.

3. When the air quality is poor because of smog and other pollutants, it's important that we remain indoors and to try not to breath too much.

Friday, February 22, 9:20am
Mayfield Elementary School
McCook, Nebraska

## Q & A session with School Officials

Q: **We believe Education is paramount. How can we better educate our children?**

A: We need to strap on our boxing gloves to help knockout illiteracy. To do that, we must contact these people in order to help them. Well, I'm proud to stand before you to tell you I've already begun the fight.

I've recently sent out comprehensive questionnaires to these people. And let me assure you, that this will be totally confidential. If you don't believe me, just ask Felix Stewart of 134 Spruce Hill Lane in Fredericksburg, Virginia. He'll tell you. Once I get these forms back I will set up a task force to alleviate this problem.

The task force I'm developing will be open 24 hours a day, 7 days a week between the hours of 3 and 5.

The name of this operation is … **T. E. A. C. H.**
It stands for **T**ogether **E**veryone **A**chieves a **L**ot **M**ore.

It no secret when I tell you that this country lacks behind other nations when it comes to reading and writing. I've recently been told that there are 6-year olds in the Far East who are already speaking Japanese. I've also heard that there are youngsters in Europe who can speak French. Yet, this country continues to fall behind. Let's face it, the United States got off to a bad start in educating its people.

300 years ago the rest of the world knew how to read and comprehend. These people knew about their History. They knew about the Magna Carta. They knew about the many works of Shakespeare. Yet, 300 years ago in this country, many Americans hadn't even a clue as to what the Declaration of Independence was all about. I blame their parents for that.

It seems that so many of us are interested only in today, and I think that's tragic. We must take pride in our heritage.

Recently, I was down in Tampa, Florida. While I was strolling along the beach, I looked out over the Pacific and thought about those young men and women who fought for our freedom as they rose up against the British forces during the bloody battles of that Civil War. They were fighting for our country.

While I was in Florida, I regret not seeing The Alamo, because that site played such an important role in our History. It was there, 135 years ago when Robert E. Lee sat down with General Mills, the cereal killer, to iron out their differences. It was a better world they wanted. A better world for their children and their children's children, as well as the children of their children, and the children of their parents. History, which began a long time ago, tells us that.

When John Philip Sousa sat down to draft the Bill of Rights, he wanted an inclusive society that would give birth to a brighter future. Thus, the Labor Party was born. In that Bill of Rights, he stated that all men are created equal. It was what America was founded upon.

Friends, I believe in that principle of Education.

I'd like to take this time to show you a letter I received from 12-year old Billy Garrett of Elmira, New York.

Billy was preparing for the National Spelling Bee competition. I offered to help him by spending many hours with Billy getting him ready for the event.

I'm very proud of Billy and feel humble that he welcomed my expertise.

'Thank You' letter from Billy Garrett to Paul Mellor after the youngster competed in the National Spelling Bee.

> DEAR MR. MELLOR,
>
> THANK YOU FOR HELLPING ME WITH MY SPELING. IT WAS A LOT OF FUN.
>
> I WAS SAD THAT I DID NOT WIN, BUT PLEESED THAT I MET VERY NISE PEEPLE.
>
> I HOPE YOU KEN HELLP ME NEKS YEAR TO.
>
> – BILLY

Tuesday, June 18, 7:45pm
Little River Methodist Church
Nashua, New Hampshire

## New Hampshire Town Hall Meeting

**Q:** **How are you going to help the little guy?**
**A:** I will raise his spirts.

**Q:** **What are your views on the homeless?**
**A:** Put them into tax shelters.

**Q:** **How can you help the people of New Hampshire?**
**A:** The people of New Hampshire are good people. From those who work in the coal mines to those who man the concessions at Niagara Falls. I'll help every New Hampshire resident. I value your friendship and I yearn for your decency. From your Green Mountains to your shining cities of Hartford and New Haven, New Hampshire is dear to my heart.

**Q:** **Is global warming a concern for you?**
**A:** Any discussion on global warming should be frozen.

**Q:** **How should we handle the Transportation Bill?**
**A:** Pay it.

**Q:** **Isn't it difficult to lift the trade embargo?**
**A:** We have no knowledge how heavy it is.

Road to the White House

Wednesday, May 14, 8:32am
New York Stock Exchange (near the back door)
New York, New York

## Q & A with Financial Advisors

Q: **Can you clarify your position on Inflation & Deregulation?**

A: Inflation and Deregulation go hand-in-hand. Why? We live in a complex world with complex issues. Society, as a whole, must tabulate these issues into a wedge of complexing measures consisting not only of a bilateral consumption of freedom and industry, but also a partnership that helps merit a reward for those involved in this process. It's important that we understand this.

To simplify, our monetary system relishes a pattern of a behavioral modification plan which is clearly defined in our system of government. It is my belief that we must plunge forward to rectify this energy of power which constantly magnetizes our thoughts, so hope and equality will remain not only coloristic, but also pro-melanistic to our judgments.

When we have all these parts working together in a state of harmonic passion, it will certainly buffer the ways in which we live. As your President, I'll fight hard for this Inflation/Deregulation process for all people.

Friday, August 31, 5:00pm
Intersection of N. St. Clair and E. Grand
Chicago, Illinois

## Q & A with Man on the Street

Q: **What are your views on Foreign Policy? And also, can you spare a dime?**

A: The United States must maintain its strength and durability. We must guard our shores against the tyranny of our allied nations, including our European neighbors of Great Britain, Austria, and Venezuela.

I worry about the Polish and their links to the outside world. I'm concerned about the Danish and how they sweet talk us, and the people of Greece who go everywhere.

We must get tough and not waffle to the Belgians, and to look past the Italian dressing to see what they are truly after.

The world is a crazy place. There are meatballs in Sweden, potato heads in Germany, and nuts in Brazil that we must constantly monitor.

Tuesday, March 3, 4:15pm
Westlake Nursing Home
Sebring, Florida

## Q & A with Residents

**Q:** **What are your thoughts about Euthanasia?**

**A:** That's a great question. I think you would need the backing of a parent or guardian, and of course, the funds. Without the funds, it would be almost impossible to pull off.

For instance, my nephew Adam traveled abroad and had those available funds.

Now to your question, it's certainly not as expensive to travel to many of those countries, but it can be costly when visiting Japan.

So, overall, I would answer YES, go for it. A Youth in Asia can only be good.

Road to the White House

```
Wednesday, February 8, 6:14pm
All Boys Network
Boise, Idaho
```

## Q & A with Board of Directors

Q: **Should businesses be required to have women on their Board of Directors?**

A: Let me get this straight. Are you asking me if businesses <u>SHOULD</u> be required or if businesses <u>BE</u> required?

Frankly, that's a very confusing question. What happens if a business doesn't have a Board of Directors, then what? And what happens if the Board of Directors is not a part of a business?

And what about the country club that I'm a member of where women aren't even allowed?

Again, I find this question very confusing.

Road to the White House

```
Thursday, April 9, 11:08am
Main Street Café (on Elm and Third)
Harrisburg, Pennsylvania
```

## Q & A with Lunch Crowd

**Q:** **Where do you stand with Government Mandates?**
**A:** Government should stay out of the personal lives of red-blooded Americans. I know a lot of successful men who have no interest in getting married or let alone date. If a man dates, that should not be the Government's concern.

**Q:** **Do you believe in Affirmative Action?**
**A:** Friends, these are the types of questions I wrestle with. I hope you join me on this crusade.

**Q:** **How do you feel about Bilingualism?**
**A:** As I've stated countless times, I believe if couples wish to take part in bilingualism, and that they're consulting adults and have been pre-tested for any bacterial contamination, they should have the blessing of the people. The Doctrine of the Holy Roman Empire, beginning in 480 BC, clearly states this.

As you may recall from your Sunday School class, it was Joseph and Isaiah who along with Mary Magdalene, assisted Moses with his ark. And how did they do it? Two by two, that's how.

Tuesday, September 15, 11:08am
Danny's Boat Sales & Service
Amesbury, Massachusetts

## Q & A with Danny

Q: **Do you support the use of hydraulic fracking to extract oil from natural resources?**

A: Has anyone here actually seen oil extracted from the ground? I didn't think so. Friend, this has been a hoax since the Truman Administration that there is oil beneath the ground.

Oil is actually a mixture of Magnesium, Selenium, and Cerium which is a chemical compound created by the rich.

Q: **Are you going to buy a boat?**

Monday, March 20, 2:10pm
Shephard's Animal Shelter
Pigeon Forge, Tennessee

## Q & A with owner Mary Alice Shephard

**Q:** **Your opponent claims you're weak on Animal Rights. How do you respond?**

**A:** I've never been afraid of controversary. That's why I met with the Animal Rights Activists at their Moose Lodge in Buffalo.

The organizer of the event was Bill Duckworth, a former boxer in the featherweight division. The meeting was like a kangaroo court, as Duckworth conducted the lion's share of the session. What he was saying was a lot of bull. He intimidated everyone with his gorilla tactics that many people were too chicken to say anything. I couldn't bear it.

His story seemed fishy as he attempted to badger and dog me with questions about allocating more funds to his cause. He said, "The turkeys in Congress need to pass the Animal Rights Protection Bill." I tried to tell him that certain bills move at a snail's pace and this one hasn't snaked its way through Congress. He didn't listen, so I barked back saying, "I'm not in Congress."

He got mad and drove off in his Jaguar realizing I wasn't going to give him any bucks.

As it turned out, he was a loan shark. He used this meeting to push his own agenda and his attitude would seal it to others as well. He was no tough guy fighting for them, but only a paper tiger who was looking out for himself.

I believe in Animal Rights. If elected, I propose they be allowed to get equal rights and join the rat race like the rest of us.

```
July 12, 9:45am
Top of the Morn to You Café
St. Joseph's, Missouri
```

## Q & A with Breakfast Patrons

Q: **The cost of health care is skyrocketing. How are you going to address this issue?**

A: With the help of Nafeesa, my 2-year old Pointer, you'll see how my 5-point plan provides solutions that will reduce medical costs by a whopping 43%.

Do away with Anesthesiologist. Instead, show patient total bill prior to going under. He'll be knocked out for hours.

Shortly after birth, doctors should remove tonsils, thus eliminating return visit.

Host a Professional Bowlers event on a hallway that is seldom in use. Sell tickets.

Save uneaten dinner rolls for another day. (Many hospitals are already doing this)

Cash in magazines from waiting rooms. (Pre-1980 are worth thousands)

Saturday, October 29, 8:05pm
Richard M. Nixon Library
Yorba Linda, California

## Q & A with The People

**Q:** **What would you say were the 3 biggest turning points for our nation?**

**A:** I've thought about this a lot. I'd have to say the 3 biggest turning points in our History are the San Francisco Earthquake of 1904, the IWCS Act of 1973, and the formation of NAF.

The most powerful of these was the **San Francisco Earthquake of 1904**. When this occurred the economy, as well as many businesses, became unstable. When prices for goods and services fell, residents couldn't get back onto their feet. Today, people don't seem to pay much attention to this event, but I find it rather odd that soon after came the Great Depression when a cold blast of air came down from Canada.

I often wonder what would had happened if the earthquake had not occurred, but it did, and it woke a lot of people up. A few years later the quake made its way to the eastern seaboard and in 1929 the Stock Market crashed. Then, many Americans started losing their jobs. The year was 1939. *Gone with the Wind* had just been released, as well as the first *Rocky* movie when times started to change.

In an interview in the New England Journal of Medicine, French President Jean-Claude Killy said America would be suffering. The reason was sugar; pure and simple. The people of Damascus and Madagascar yearned for our sugar, but they didn't want to pay the tax. For years they bickered. Until a little girl from Kansas named Susan B. Anthony made a simple plea. It was she who coined the phrase, "The Buck Stops Here." It was a statement that earned Miss Anthony a Tony Award, but more importantly gave us back our dignity. The people of Jerusalem and Jericho understood that, and when Navy ships approached the Baltic Sea under the command of Captain Crunch, peace was at hand. The US Government restored order reprimanding Clara Barton and her Camp Fire Girls, and although Sitting Bull never stood trial for what he did, America's role in the new world order had begun.

The second important event facing this nation was the **IWCS Act of 1973**. This Act, I believe, affected more working Americans than anything I have seen in the last 100 years.

IWCS or **I**ndividually **W**rapped **C**heese Slices, was a movement that was well on its way long before the 1970's.

Cheese has always been one of our leading byproducts. In fact, historians now say that this was the only kind of food many families consumed. They learned this by studying early photographs and then conducting countless interviews asking families as to what they were saying prior to the taking of the picture.

In the early 1300's during the Byzantine Period, Marco Polo asked Queen Isabella of Spain if he could carry the product to North America. The Queen agreed.

In May, shortly before Daylight Saving Time, Polo fled Madrid on a slow boat to China. However, under the direction of Christopher Columbus they went off course arriving in New York's Times Square several months later. Polo then traded pelts with the Indians who just so happened to be in town playing the Yankees that day.

After several weeks, Polo headed west along the Pennsylvania Turnpike on his way to the Oregon Trail in hopes of tracing the route taken by Rodgers and Hammerstein some years earlier, as members of the Pony Express. But the trip failed, and Polo settled in what is now Wisconsin, and it was there many years later that the delicacy became individually wrapped. Shortly thereafter relations with China opened.

A lot of credit was given to Richard Nixon, but I doubt it would had been possible if it weren't for that young Spaniard named Marco Polo.

The third biggest turning point in our History happened in the 20$^{th}$ Century with the formation of **NAF**, or Neighborhood Association Fees. Why, I ask.

June 26, 6:27pm
Clancy's Bar & Grill
Fergus Falls, Minnesota

## Q & A with Concerned Citizens

**Q:** What is your stance on abortion?
**A:** This issue concerns me very much.

**Q:** Do you support a universal basic income program?
**A:** Say what???

**Q:** Should the U.S. raise or lower the tax rate for corporations?
**A:** Yes.

**Q:** Should the electoral college be abolished?
**A:** Only if we abolish ballots from New York City, Chicago, and Los Angeles.

**Q:** Should a photo ID be required to vote?
**A:** Only if the voter is good-looking.

**Q:** Should the U.S. expand offshore oil drilling?
**A:** In which direction? More out to sea or more inland?

**Q:** Should the government increase environmental regulations to prevent climate change?
**A:** Government should regulate everything so everyone will be forced to remain at home. Therefore, no driving cars, busses, and the economy.

May 4, 3:12pm
Ray's Barber Shop
Hendersonville, North Carolina

## Q & A with Long-Haired Folks

**Q:** **Should universities provide 'safe spaces' for students?**

**A:** Of course. It's not fair that we send our precious children off to college in a land that is unfamiliar to them. Our children must continue to feel safe and nurtured without being exposed to ideologies that are different from their own beliefs.

When my great grandfather attended Woodstock prior to World War I, he was appalled to what he was seeing. The drugs, the alcohol, the free sex was in his words, mortifying. During his 3$^{rd}$ day at the festival, he said it was even worse. His photographs confirm this.

My great grandfather isn't with us anymore and I wonder if his experience at Woodstock had something to do with that.

I firmly believe that if my great granddad had a 'safe space' things might had been different.

Road to the White House

January 9, 10:40am
Mission Valley High School
San Marcos, Texas

## Q & A with Townspeople

Q: Do you believe sports betting should be legal?

A: Funny you should ask. I just heard from a couple of Texas Rangers, twins actually, who think it should be legal to gamble on sports. But keep in mind, these were only rangers who believed in what they were saying. They weren't royals or kings, but only a couple of guys who like sports.

I've also heard from the religious community who say sports betting should not be legalized. One cardinal in particular, a true patriot who's a New York giant, says his congregation says 'No' to gambling. Why? Spending habits change. Bills add up and credit cards come out as everyone becomes a charger.

I side with the brave ancient mariner, an islander who spurs me on with his nuggets of wisdom. As far as his choice of clothing is concerned, well that's another story. He wore white socks and red socks, yet the rest of his clothing was a combination of reds and browns and two blue jackets. But he was a trail blazer and I listened and took notes as any cub reporter would do.

He told me that he set out to be a hair stylist, but one day after listening to Celtic music, he put down his clippers to become a sports junkie. Yes, he took a lot of heat from his cavalier attitude, but he did what he thought was right. Sports betting changed his life. For the good? We may never know, but no doubt he was a warrior, a maverick if you will, who lived life to its fullest, who courted many women, fielded many questions, covered all the bases, and had a ball. That my friends, is the icing on the cake.

```
October 6, 6:30pm
The Rec Center
Charlahoo, Kansas
```

## Q & A with The Good People of Utah

**Q:** **Do you support Affirmative Action programs?**

**A:** While fishing off the pier in Galilee, Rhode Island, I questioned whether I needed a fishing license.

## Closing Remarks

Friends, I've travelled all across the United States listening to the hopes and dreams of our people. Recently, I was in Michigan's capital city, and while I was in Topeka, I met with an 82-year old woman named GG Goldsmith.

She said she grew up as a poor child on the outskirts of Memphis, Tennessee. She said each night before she went to bed she would open her window, lean out, and see Lady Liberty with her hand held high. She said living so close to the Statue of Liberty gave her hope that she could be someone.

The year was 1921, right at the turn of the century, when her father Jack, named after President Kennedy, worked two jobs. From 8 to 5 he would pick tobacco, even though he had a strong urge to chew it. After his days in the field he would head off to his other job as a computer programmer.

GG told me that the family grew up without electricity. When she told me that I wondered about all those nights when the family had to gather candle after candle in order to watch television This would devastate most families, but for GG it was a way out.

The year was 1941 during the Eisenhower Administration when she got accepted to the Naval Academy in Minneapolis, and it was there that she learned it's a whole lot cheaper to dial direct than using an operator when making a long-distance call.

Friends, that's the kind of America I envision.

You see, most politicians are only concerned about themselves while they plug their own agenda and their own book ($10, two for $20).

Friends, we need politicians like the ones of old, such as Abraham Lincoln, John Quincy Adams, and George Jefferson who fought for what was right. And friends, I'm right, and sometimes a little left of center depending upon my audience. I ask for your vote!

The Office of the Presidency is one I'd like to hold;
    to be in charge of the people and say what's needed to be told.

I'd sit in the Oval Office and make decisions every day;
    about taxes and cutbacks, and if school kids ought to pray.

I'd go out to see the people, to tell them what I think;
    and then attend the fundraisers with good food and lots to drink.

I'd cut ribbons to open businesses and do all the ceremonial stuff;
    like telling them how much they mean to me and speaking off the cuff.

I'd tell the people what they wanted to hear, and they'd think of me as kind;
    and then right after the election, I'd tell them, "I changed my mind."

I'd show concern for everyone, sometimes I'd even cry;
    people would think I'm real sincere and my ratings would go high.

I'd be a President who is tough on crime and I'd be backed
by the F.O.P.
    I'd promise the people justice and keep the criminals
    from going free.


I'd set out to help the poor, like spreading out the wealth;
    and if anyone was without insurance, I'd give them all
    free health.


I'd stay in touch with all the people through letters and
through faxes;
    saying, "I feel your pain" and I'd be out to lower taxes.


I'd tell the people I'm working hard to lower the national
debt;
    and when it's time for re-election, I'd say, "Stick with
    me. I'm not finished yet."


Yes, this job would be ideal for me, and it's one I'd like
to have;
    living in that big white house on Pennsylvania Ave.


Of course, I cannot do it without your help, so I'm here to
make a plea;
    the next time you're in the voting booth, I beg you, push
    that lever down for me.

## Other books by Paul Mellor

**Finding the Keys**
…for Remembering Anything (305 pages)

**STOP Studying So Much**
Achieve better grades with half the study (136 pages)

**How to Remember Bible Verses**
Perfect companion to your Bible (124 pages)

**Summer in the Saddle**
Bike ride across America (267 pages)

**You're Almost There**
Running a marathon in 50 states (376 pages)

**Pathway to the Podium**
Life as a Professional Speaker (232 pages)

**You Have the Right to Remember**
Memory skills for law enforcement (240 pages)

**Memory Skills for Lawyers**
How to remember case law and speaking without notes (266 Pages)

For information on Paul Mellor's books and seminars, visit his website at
# www.mellormemory.com

www.ingramcontent.com/pod-product-compliance
Lightning Source LLC
Chambersburg PA
CBHW071804040426
42446CB00012B/2702